Sit There & Move!

Sit There & Move! **Offers a variety of easy chair exercises that can be done in the comfort of your home or absolutely anywhere at anytime.**

Each exercise can be done 10-12 times or 10-12 reps and up to 5 sets for a total of 50-60 times per exercise.

FYI:

There are 7 stretching / warm-up exercises
&
10 chair exercises included in this workout.

Just follow along with the instructions in this book and enjoy doing something that's easy to naturally strengthen your joints, as well as improve your mental and physical well-being.

Please modify the exercises to fit your levels of
physical stamina or ability. On some days you might
be able to do less or more of these.
The main thing is to show up every day and do this!

3-5 lb hand weights & a stretch band is recommended but are not required. Simply complete these exercises without using the hand weights or stretch band.

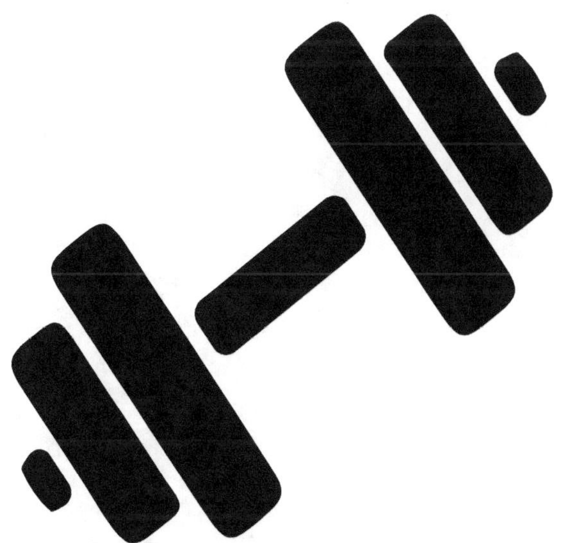

Food for thought:

Changing your habits will change your life!

That's it....Let's Go!

Step 1

Stretching / Warm-up

Sit up straight, raise your right arm to gently press
the left side of your head to the right.
Hold for 15 seconds. Repeat on opposite side.
Repeat for 3 times on each side.

While still being seated, bring your right arm
across your body & hold your arm
at the elbow with your left hand.
Gently press your elbow
to stretch your arm. Hold for 15 seconds.
Repeat on opposite side.
Repeat for 3 times on each side.

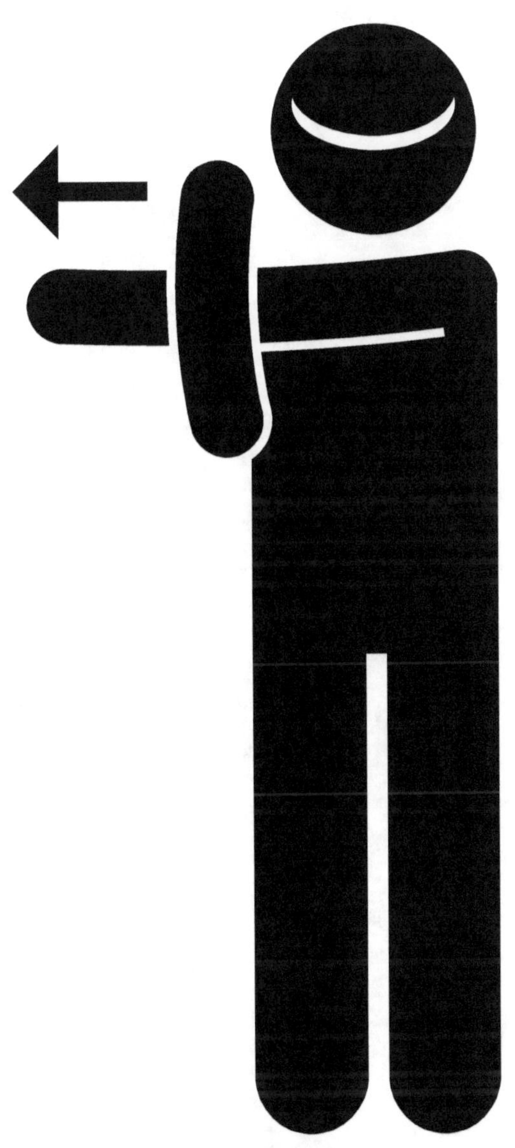

Place your left hand on your right knee as shown below.
Twist your upper body to the right to
look over your right shoulder.
Hold for 15 seconds. Repeat on opposite side.
Repeat for 3 times on each side.

Get a firm grip on the back of your chair then
raise the back of your heels to stand on your toes.
Hold for 15 seconds then place your feet
flat on the floor. Repeat for 3 times.

Sit up straight, raise your arms above your head, then lean to the left as far as you can go. Hold for 15 seconds then sit up straight & repeat on opposite side. Do this for 3 times on each side.

Sit up straight then lean forward to grab
your feet or ankles. Hold for 15 seconds then sit up
straight & repeat for 3 times.

Place your right arm over your head, lean to the
left until you feel a slight pull in your
left side & back.
Stretch your right leg out as far as you can go.
Hold for 15 seconds.
Repeat on opposite side.
Repeat for 3 times on each side.

Hooray!

The stretching & warm-up session is complete.

Step 2

Let's Do This!

Food for thought:

You are your best source of motivation!

#1 - Overhead Arm Extensions

Grab your 3-5 lb hand weights. Sit up straight. Extend
your right arm over your head then slowly
lower your arm.
Repeat this for 10-12 times then switch sides for
10-12 more times.

#2 - Knee Lifts

Sit up straight then lean towards your right
knee to touch your left elbow with your right knee.
Repeat this for 12 times then
switch sides for 12 more times.

#3 - Touch Your Feet

Sit up straight, raise your right arm then lean
towards the side of your left foot
with your left hand.
Bend as low as you can to touch
the side of your left foot.
Repeat this for 12 times then switch
sides for 12 more times.

#4 - Arm Pulls

Grab your stretch band.
Sit on the middle of your chair.
Wrap your stretch band around
the bottom of your feet.
Grab the bands with both hands & extend your
legs in front of you.
Sit up straight then pull back with both arms.
Repeat for 10-12 times.

#5 - Leg Raises

Use the front or back of your chair.
Get a firm grip on the front or back of the chair.
Lean into a comfortable position.
Raise & lower your right leg.
Repeat this for 10-12 times then switch sides
for 10-12 more times.

#6 - Chair Lunge

Hold on to the back of the chair.
Raise your right arm with your right knee bent.
Slightly squat with your left leg bent
(as pictured below),
then stand while lowering your right arm.
Repeat this for 10-12 times then switch sides
for 10-12 more times.

#7 - Jog In Place

Use the front or back of your chair.
Get a firm grip on the front or back of the chair.
Lean into a comfortable position.
Step forward with your right leg then
alternate by stepping forward with your left leg.
Do this as fast as you can.
Repeat this for 24 times (12 times on each side).

#8 - Seated Jumping Jacks

Sit on the middle of your chair.
Lift your arms above your
head & open your legs as wide as you can.
Bring your arms down while
bringing your legs together.
Repeat for 10-12 times.

#9 - Chair Squats

Stand in front of your chair.
Extend your arms in front of you
then squat as low as you can.
Return to the standing position
& repeat for 10-12 times.

#10 - Arm & Back Weight Lift

While still using your 3-5 lb hand weights.
Sit on the middle of your seat.
Stretch your right arm behind you (as pictured).
Lean down to bring the hand weight
to the floor with your left hand
then sit up straight.
Bring your right arm to you right side
while bringing the hand weight to your lap.
Repeat this for 12 times then switch sides
for 12 more times.

Step 3

Repeat the exercises in Step 2
for up to 4 more times!

Exercises Recap

#1 - Overhead Arm Extensions

#2 - Knee Lifts

#3 - Touch Your Feet

#4 - Arm Pulls

#5 - Leg Raises

#6 - Chair Lunge

#7 - Jog In Place

#8 - Seated Jumping Jacks

#9 - Chair Squats

#10 - Arm & Back Weight Lift

Step 4 - Cool Down

Complete these 5 quick cool down stretches & you're done!

Sit up straight, raise your right arm to gently press the left side of your head to the right. Hold for 15 seconds. Repeat on opposite side. Repeat for 3 times on each side.

**While still being seated, bring your
right arm across your body &
hold your arm at the elbow with
your left hand. Gently press your elbow
to stretch your arm. Hold for 15 seconds.
Repeat on opposite side.
Repeat for 3 times on each side.**

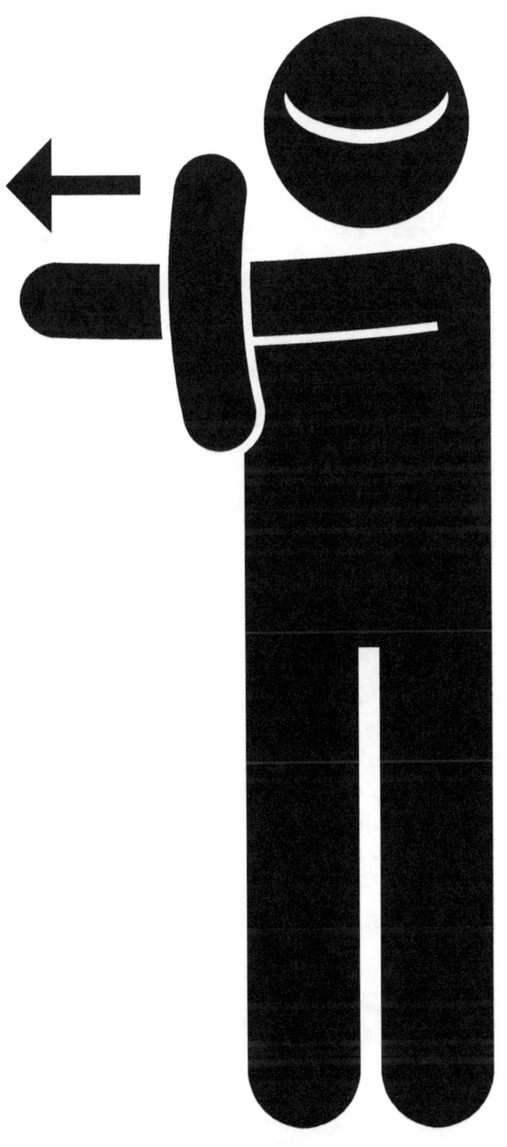

Place your left hand on your right knee
(as pictured below).
Twist your upper body to the right to look over your
right shoulder. Hold for 15 seconds.
Repeat on opposite side.
Repeat for 3 times on each side.

Sit up straight, raise your arms above your head,
then lean to the left as far as you can go.
Hold for 15 seconds then sit up straight &
repeat on opposite side.
Do this for 3 times on each side.

Sit up straight then lean forward to
grab your feet or ankles.
Hold for 15 seconds then sit up straight &
repeat for 3 times.

Hooray!

You did it....

You did an amazing job & should be very proud of yourself.

Food for thought:

When you invest in your own spiritual, mental, emotional, intellectual & physical wellbeing you are arming yourself to be the very best that you can be.